Children's Songs for Ukulele Strummers

38 Fun Songs for Singing, Playing and Listening

To access audio visit:
www.halleonard.com/mylibrary

Enter Code
5705-6537-9765-8420

ISBN 978-1-4768-1275-5

HAL•LEONARD®
7777 W. BLUEMOUND RD. P.O. BOX 13819 MILWAUKEE, WI 53213

Visit Hal Leonard Online at
www.halleonard.com

Traditional

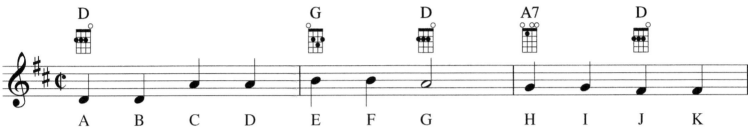

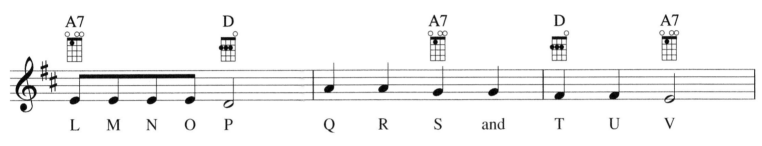

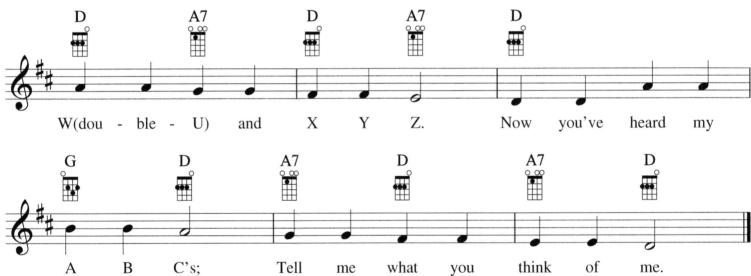

(Oh, My Darling) Clementine

Words and Music by PERCY MONTROSE

Any Dream Will Do

from JOSEPH AND THE AMAZING
TECHNICOLOR® DREAMCOAT
Music by ANDREW LLOYD WEBBER
Lyrics by TIM RICE

Note: Each time a letter of BINGO is deleted in the lyric, clap your hands in place of singing the letter.

Traditional

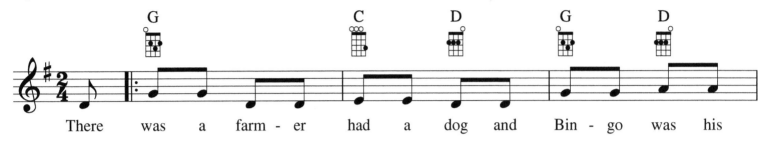

There was a farm-er had a dog and Bin-go was his

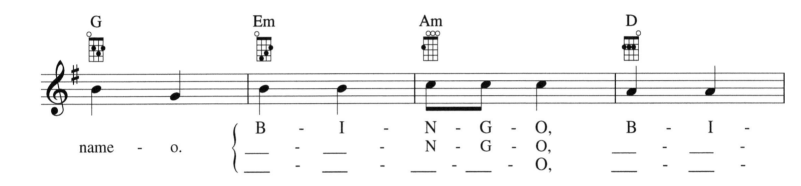

name - o. { B - I - N - G - O, B - I -
___ - ___ - N - G - O,
___ - ___ - ___ - ___ - O,   ___ - ___ -

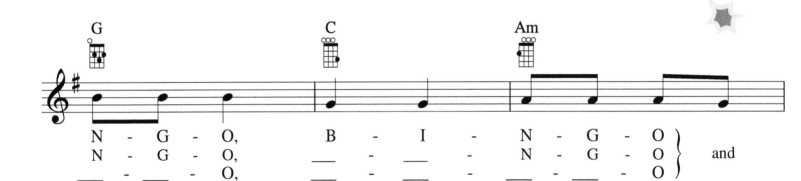

N - G - O, B - I - N - G - O
N - G - O, ___ - ___ - N - G - O } and
___ - ___ - O, ___ - ___ - ___ - ___ - O

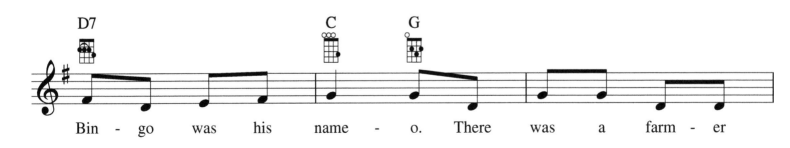

Bin - go was his name - o. There was a farm - er

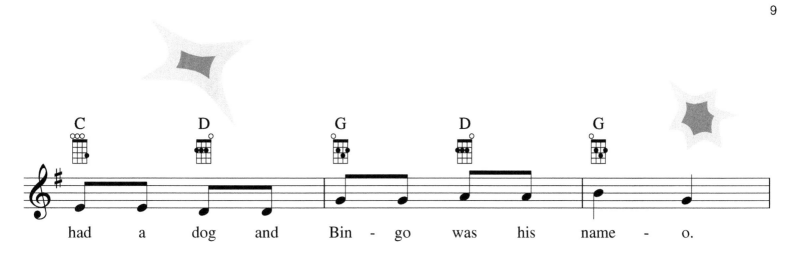

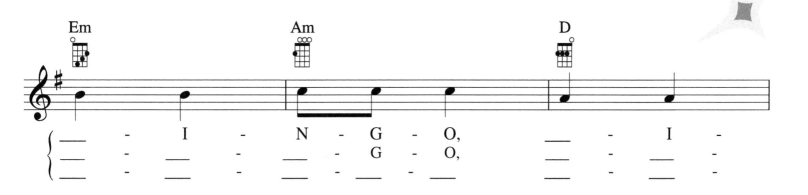

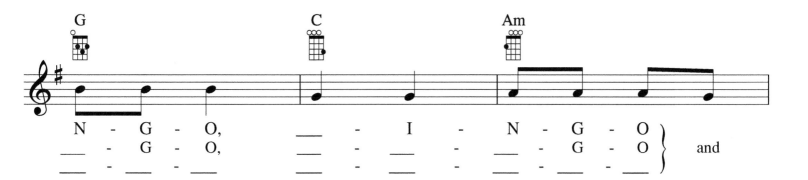

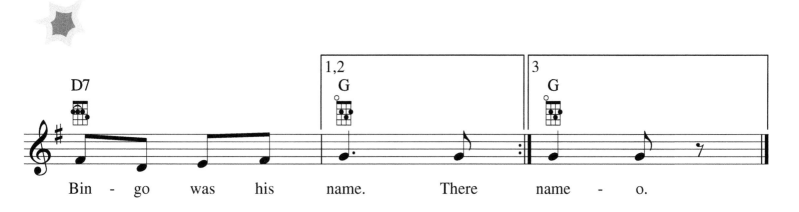

9

BOB THE BUILDER

"Intro Theme Song"
Words and Music by PAUL JOYCE

Scoop, Muck and Diz - zy   and Ro - ley too; __   Lof - ty and Wen - dy
Time   to   get bus - y; such a   lot   to   do, __   build - ing and fix - ing 'til it's

join   the crew. __   Bob   and   the   gang   have   so   much   fun ___
good   as   new. __   Bob   and   the   gang   make a   real - ly   good   sound, __

work - ing   to - geth - er   to   get   the   job   done. }   Bob   the   Build - er.
work - ing   all   day   'til   the   sun __   goes   down. }

(Can   we   fix   it?)   Bob   the   Build - er.   (Yes,   we   can!)

Bob   the   Build - er.   (Can   we   fix   it?)   Bob   the   Build - er.   (Yes,   we   can!)

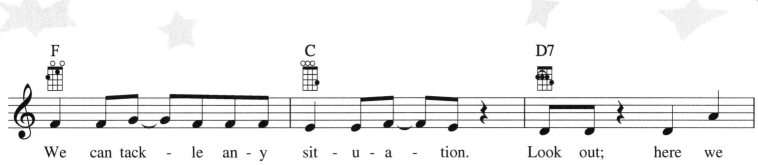

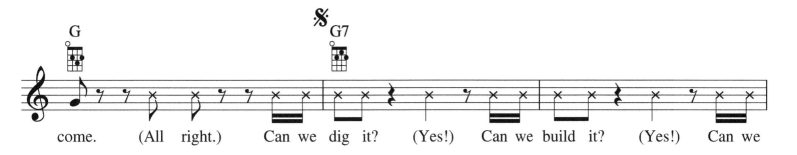

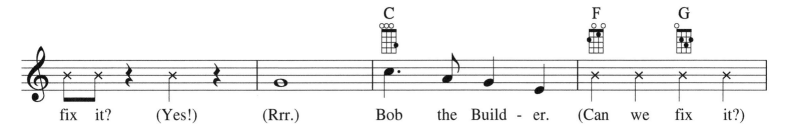

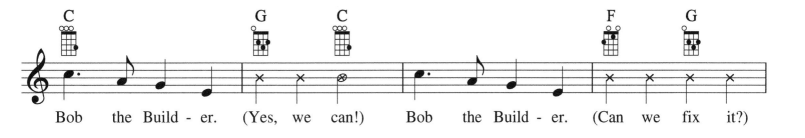

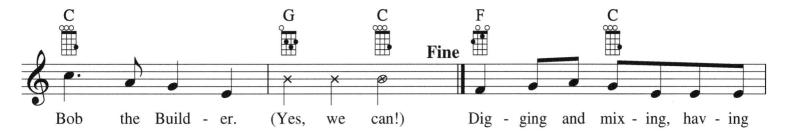

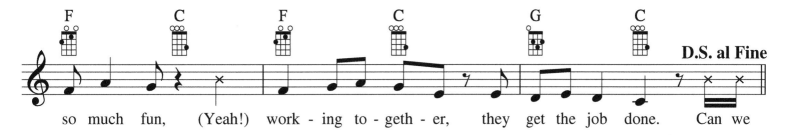

CANDLE ON THE WATER

from Walt Disney's PETE'S DRAGON

Words and Music by AL KASHA
and JOEL HIRSCHHORN

Spiritually

I'll be your can-dle on the wa-ter, my love for you will al-ways
I'll be your can-dle on the wa-ter, 'til ev-'ry wave is warm and

burn. I know you're lost and drift-ing, but the clouds are lift-ing.
bright. My soul is there be-side you, let this can-dle guide you.

Don't give up you have some-where to turn.
Soon you'll see a gold-en stream of light. A cold and friend-less tide has

found you, don't let the storm-y dark-ness pull you down. I'll paint a ray of hope a-

Do-Re-Mi

from THE SOUND OF MUSIC
Lyrics by OSCAR HAMMERSTEIN II
Music by RICHARD RODGERS

Down by the Station

Traditional

Down by the sta-tion ear-ly in the morn-ing,

See the lit-tle puf-fer-bil-lies all in a row.

See the en-gine driv-er pull the lit-tle han-dle.

Choo! Choo! Toot! Toot! Off they go!

Eensy Weensy Spider

Traditional

Een - sy, ween - sy spi - der went up the wa - ter spout. Down came the rain and washed the spi - der out. Out came the sun and dried up all the rain, And the een - sy, ween - sy spi - der went up the spout a - gain.

For He's a Jolly Good Fellow

Traditional

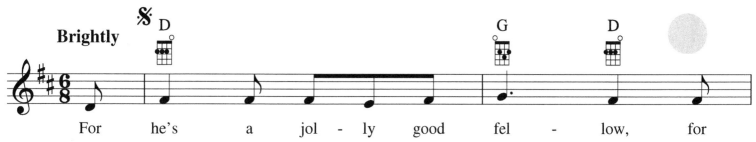

Brightly

For he's a jol - ly good fel - low, for

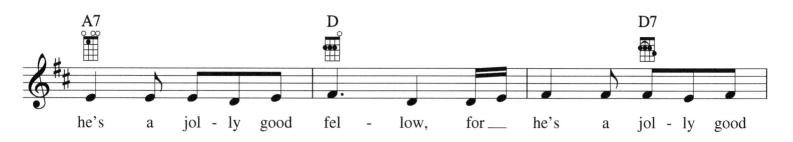

he's a jol - ly good fel - low, for ___ he's a jol - ly good

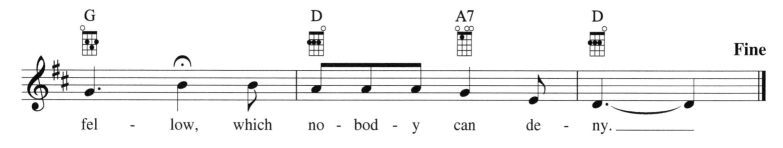

fel - low, which no - bod - y can de - ny. ___

Fine

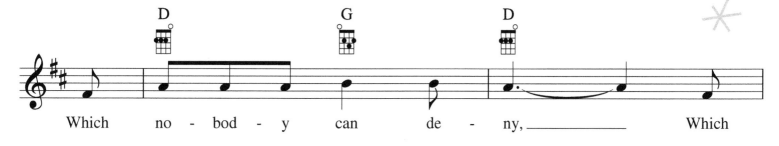

Which no - bod - y can de - ny, ___ Which

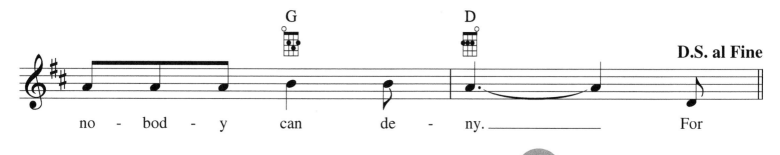

D.S. al Fine

no - bod - y can de - ny. ___ For

Frère Jacques (Are You Sleeping?)

Traditional

Frè - re Jac - ques, Frè - re Jac - ques,
Are you sleep - ing? Are you sleep - ing?

Dor - mez - vous? Dor - mez - vous? son - nez les ma -
Broth - er John, Broth - er John, morn - ing bells are

ti - nes, son - nez les ma - ti - nes:
ring - ing, morn - ing bells are ring - ing:

Ding, din, don! Ding, din, don!
Ding, din, dang, dong! Ding, din, dang, dong!

The Hokey Pokey

Words and Music by CHARLES P. MACAK,
TAFFT BAKER and LARRY LaPRISE

Additional Lyrics

*2nd time: left foot
*3rd time: right arm
*4th time: left arm
*5th time: right elbow
*6th time: left elbow

*7th time: head
*8th time: right hip
*9th time: left hip
*10th time: whole self

Home on the Range

Lyrics by DR. BREWSTER HIGLEY
Music by DAN KELLY

1. Oh, give me a home where the buf - fa - lo
2. How oft - en at night when the heav - ens are
3. Where the air is so pure, the ___ zeph - yrs so
4. Oh, I love those wild flow'rs in this dear land of

roam, Where the deer and the an - te - lope play, ___
bright with the light from the glit - ter - ing stars, ___
free, the ___ light breez - es so balm - y and light. ___
ours. The ___ cur - lew, I love to hear scream. ___

___ Where sel - dom is heard a dis - cour - ag - ing
___ have I stood there a - mazed and ___ asked as I
___ That I would not ex - change my ___ home on the
___ And I love the white rocks and the an - te - lope

word, And the skies are not cloud - y all day. ___
gazed, if their glo - ry ex - ceeds that of ours. ___
range for ___ all of the cit - ies so bright. ___
flocks, that ___ graze on the moun - tain - tops green. ___

I've Been Working on the Railroad

American Folksong

If You're Happy and You Know It

Words and Music by L. SMITH

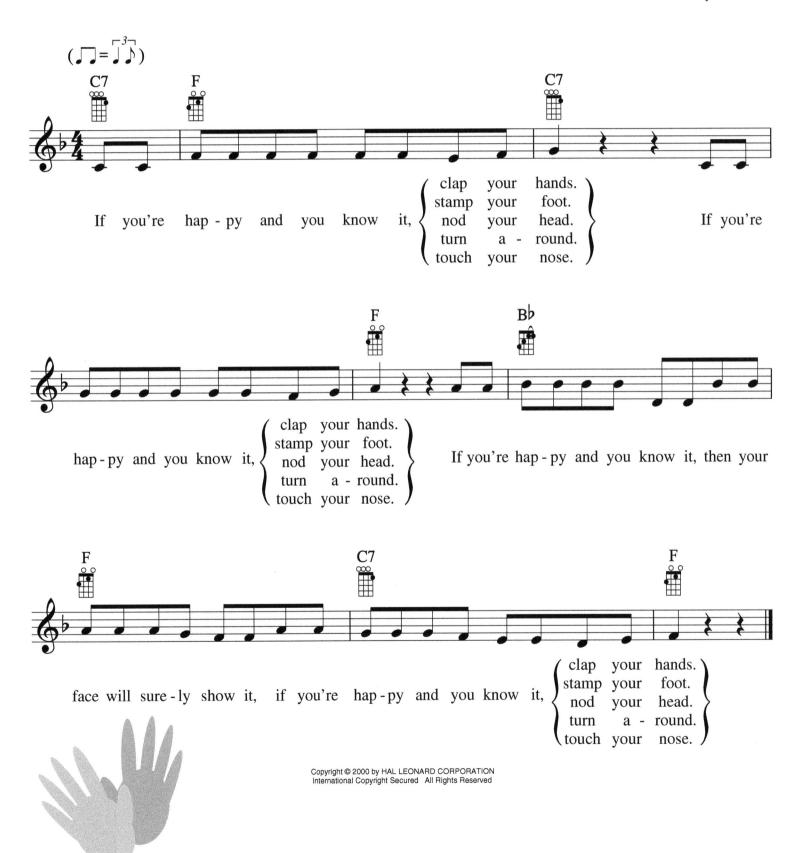

IT'S A SMALL WORLD

from Disneyland Resort® and Magic Kingdom® Park
Words and Music by RICHARD M. SHERMAN
and ROBERT B. SHERMAN

KUM BA YAH

Traditional Spiritual

1. Kum ba yah, my Lord, Kum ba yah. Kum ba
2. Some - one's pray - in', Lord, Kum ba yah. Some - one's

3.-6. *(See additional lyrics)*

yah, my Lord, Kum ba yah. Kum ba yah, my Lord, Kum ba
pray - in', Lord, Kum ba yah. Someone's pray - in', Lord, Kum ba

yah. Oh, Lord, _____ Kum ba yah.
yah. Oh, Lord, _____ Kum ba yah.

Additional Lyrics

3. Someone's singin', Lord, Kum ba yah...
4. Someone's cryin', Lord, Kum ba yah...
5. Someone's dancin', Lord, Kum ba yah...
6. Someone's shoutin', Lord, Kum ba yah...

Traditional

D

Lon - don Bridge is fall - ing down,
Take the key and lock her up,
Build it up with silver and gold,

A7 ... **D**

fall - ing down, fall - ing down. Lon - don Bridge is
lock her up, lock her up. Take the key and
silver and gold, silver and gold. Build it up with

A7 **D**

fall - ing down, ⎫
lock her up, ⎬ my fair la - dy - o.
silver and gold, ⎭

MICHAEL ROW THE BOAT ASHORE

Traditional Folksong

1. Mi - chael, row the boat a - shore, al - le - lu -
2.-5. *(See additional lyrics)*

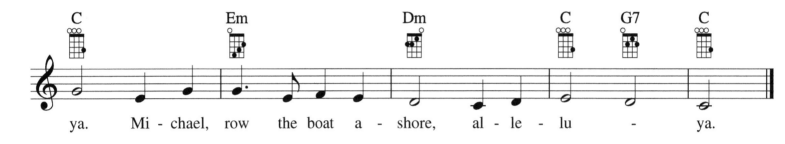

ya. Mi - chael, row the boat a - shore, al - le - lu - ya.

Additional Lyrics

2. Sister, help to trim the sail...

3. Michael's boat is a gospel boat...

4. Jordan River is chilly and cold...
   Chills the body but warms the soul...

5. Jordan River is deep and wide...
   Meet my mother on the other side...

MICKEY MOUSE MARCH

from Walt Disney's
THE MICKEY MOUSE CLUB
Words and Music by
JIMMIE DODD

The Muffin Man

Traditional

F   Gm7   F   B♭   G7

Do you know the muf - fin man, the muf - fin man, the

C7   F   Gm7   F   B♭6   C7

muf - fin man? Do you know the muf - fin man who lives in Dru - ry

F   Gm7   F   B♭   G7

Lane? Yes, we know the muf - fin man, the muf - fin man, the

C7   F   Gm7   F   B♭6   C7   F

muf - fin man. Yes, we know the muf - fin man who lives in Dru - ry Lane.

My Bonnie Lies Over the Ocean

Traditional

My Bon - nie lies o - ver the o - cean, _____ my Bon - nie lies

o - ver the sea. _____ My Bon - nie lies o - ver the o - cean, ___

oh bring back my Bon - nie to me. _____ Bring

back, bring back, bring back my Bon - nie to me, to me.

Bring back, bring back, oh bring back my Bon - nie to me. _____

My Favorite Things

from THE SOUND OF MUSIC
Lyrics by OSCAR HAMMERSTEIN II
Music by RICHARD RODGERS

Lively, with spirit

Rain - drops on ros - es and whis - kers on kit - tens. Bright cop - per
Cream col - ored po - nies and crisp ap - ple stru - dels. Door - bells and

ket - tles and warm wool - en mit - tens. Brown pa - per pack - ag - es
sleigh-bells and schnitz - el with noo - dles. Wild geese that fly with the

tied up with string, ⎫ these are a few of my fa - vor - ite
moon on their wings, ⎭

things. Girls in white dress - es with

Oh! Susanna

Words and Music by
STEPHEN C. FOSTER

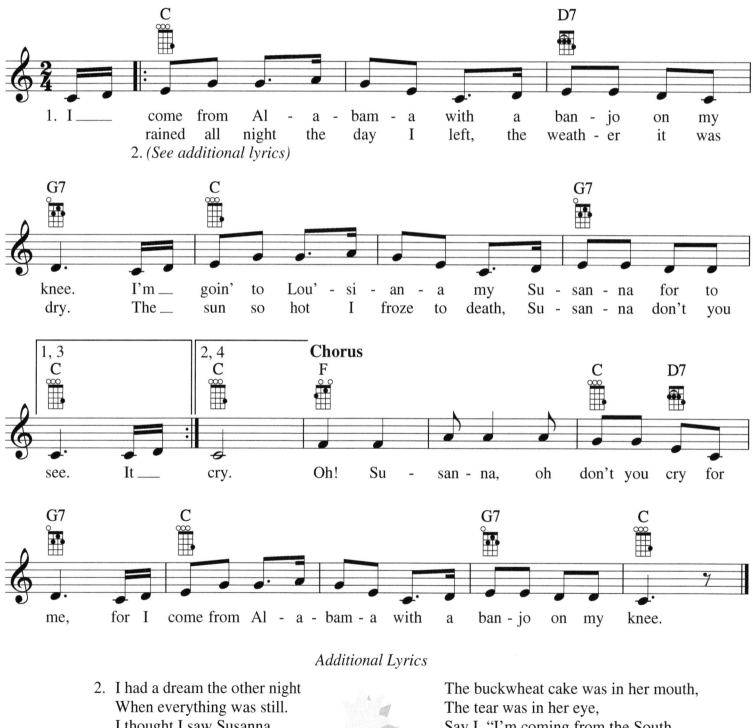

1. I ____ come from Al - a - bam - a with a ban - jo on my
rained all night the day I left, the weath - er it was
2. *(See additional lyrics)*

knee. I'm ___ goin' to Lou' - si - an - a my Su - san - na for to
dry. The ___ sun so hot I froze to death, Su - san - na don't you

1, 3
see. It ___

2, 4 **Chorus**
cry. Oh! Su - san - na, oh don't you cry for

me, for I come from Al - a - bam - a with a ban - jo on my knee.

Additional Lyrics

2. I had a dream the other night
When everything was still.
I thought I saw Susanna
A-coming down the hill.

The buckwheat cake was in her mouth,
The tear was in her eye,
Say I, "I'm coming from the South,
Susanna, don't you cry."
Chorus

Traditional Children's Song

1. Old Mac-Don-ald had a farm E - I - E - I - O! And
2.-10. *(See additional lyrics)*

on this farm he had a duck, E - I - E - I - O! With a quack-quack here, and a

quack-quack there, here a quack, there a quack, ev-'ry-where a quack, quack.

Old Mac-Don-ald had a farm, E - I - E - I - O!

Additional Lyrics

2. Old MacDonald had a farm,
E-I-E-I-O!
And on this farm he had a chick,
E-I-E-I-O!
With a chick, chick here,
And a chick, chick there,
Here a chick, there a chick,
Everywhere a chick, chick.
Old MacDonald had a farm,
E-I-E-I-O!

Other verses:

3. Cow - moo, moo
4. Dog - bow, bow
5. Pig - oink, oink
6. Rooster - cock-a-doodle, cock-a-doodle
7. Turkey - gobble, gobble
8. Cat - meow, meow
9. Horse - neigh, neigh
10. Donkey - hee-haw, hee-haw

POLLY WOLLY DOODLE

Traditional American Minstrel Song

1. Oh, I went down South for to see my Sal, sing-ing
2. Sal she is a ____ maid - en fair, sing-ing
3. grass - hop - per sit - tin' on a rail - road track, sing-ing

4.-6. *(See additional lyrics)*

pol - ly - wol - ly - doo - dle all the day. My ___ Sal she is a
pol - ly - wol - ly - doo - dle all the day. With ___ curl - y eyes and
pol - ly - wol - ly - doo - dle all the day. A - pick - in' his teeth with a

Chorus

spunk - y gal, sing - ing pol - ly - wol - ly - doo - dle all the day.
laugh - ing hair, sing - ing pol - ly - wol - ly - doo - dle all the day.
car - pet tack, sing - ing pol - ly - wol - ly - doo - dle all the day.

Fare thee

well, fare thee well, fare thee well, my fair - y fay. For I'm

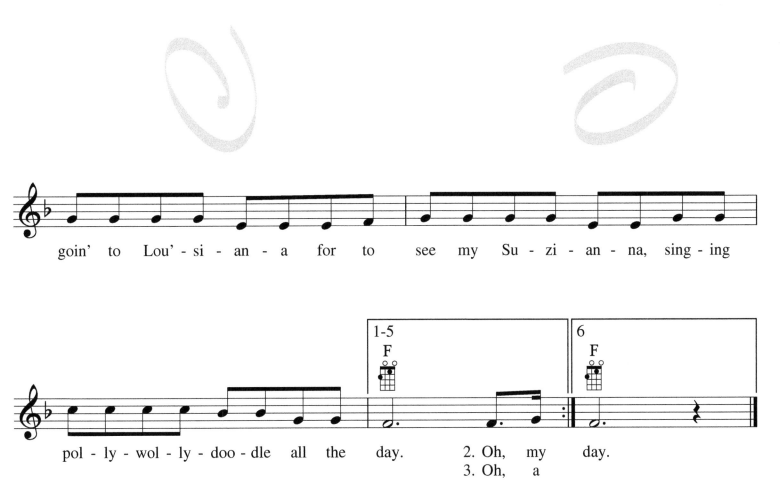

goin' to Lou' - si - an - a   for   to   see   my   Su - zi - an - na,   sing - ing

1-5
F

6
F

pol - ly - wol - ly - doo - dle   all   the   day.   2. Oh,   my   day.
3. Oh,   a

Additional Lyrics

4. Oh, I went to bed, but it wasn't no use,
    Singing polly-wolly-doodle all the day.
    My feet stuck out like a chicken roost,
    Singing polly-wolly-doodle all the day.
    Chorus

5. Behind the barn down on my knees,
    Singing polly-wolly-doodle all the day.
    I thought I heard a chicken sneeze,
    Singing polly-wolly-doodle all the day.
    Chorus

6. He sneezed so hard with the whooping cough,
    Singing polly-wolly-doodle all the day.
    He sneezed his head and tail right off,
    Singing polly-wolly-doodle all the day.
    Chorus

Puff the Magic Dragon

Words and Music by
LENNY LIPTON
and PETER YARROW

Moderately, in 2

1. Puff the mag-ic drag-on lived by ___ the sea and
2.-4. *See additional lyrics*

frol-icked in ___ the au-tumn mist ___ in a land called Hon-a-lee. ___

Lit-tle Jack-ie Pa-per loved that ras-cal Puff and brought him strings and

Chorus

seal-ing wax ___ and oth-er fan-cy stuff. Oh! Puff the Mag-ic Drag-on

lived by ___ the sea and frol-icked in ___ the au-tumn mist ___ in a

Additional Lyrics

2. Together they would travel on a boat with billowed sail.
   Jackie kept a lookout perched on Puff's gigantic tail.
   Noble kings and princes would bow whene'er they came.
   Pirate ships would low'r their flag when Puff roared out his name. Oh! *(To Chorus)*

3. A dragon lives forever, but not so little boys.
   Painted wings and giant rings make way for other toys.
   One gray night it happened, Jackie Paper came no more,
   And Puff that mighty dragon, he ceased his fearless roar. Oh! *(To Chorus)*

4. His head was bent in sorrow, green tears fell like rain.
   Puff no longer went to play along the Cherry Lane.
   Without his lifelong friend, Puff could not be brave,
   So Puff that mighty dragon sadly slipped into his cave. Oh! *(To Chorus)*

THE RAINBOW CONNECTION

from THE MUPPET MOVIE
Words and Music by PAUL WILLIAMS
and KENNETH L. ASCHER

Flowing Waltz tempo

1. Why are there so man-y songs a-bout rain-bows, and what's on the
2. Who said that ev-'ry wish would be heard and an-swered when wished on the
3. *(See additional lyrics)*

oth-er side?____ Rain-bows are vi-sions,_ but on-ly il-lu-sions, and
morn-ing star?____ Some-bod-y thought of that, and some-one be-lieved it;

rain-bows have noth-ing to hide._____ So we've been told, and some
Look what it's done_ so far._____ What's so a-maz-ing that

choose to be-lieve it; I know they're wrong; wait and see._____
keeps us star-gaz-ing, and what do we think we might see?_____

Additional Lyrics

3. Have you been half asleep and have you heard voices?
    I've heard them calling my name.
    Is this the sweet sound that calls the young sailors?
    The voice might be one and the same.
    I've heard it too many times to ignore it.
    It's something I'm s'posed to be.
    Someday we'll find it,
    The rainbow connection;
    The lovers, the dreamers and me.

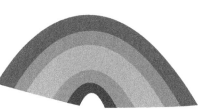

Row, Row, Row Your Boat

Traditional

Row, row, row your boat, gen - tly down the stream. Mer - ri - ly, mer - ri - ly, mer - ri - ly, mer - ri - ly, life is but a dream.

She'll Be Comin' 'Round the Mountain

Traditional

1. She'll be com-in' 'round the moun-tain when she comes, *(when she comes.)* She'll be
2.-4. *(See additional lyrics)*

com-in' 'round the moun-tain when she comes, *(when she comes.)* She'll be

com-in' 'round the moun-tain, she'll be com-in' 'round the moun-tain, she'll be

com-in' 'round the moun-tain when she comes. _____

Additional Lyrics

2. She'll be drivin' six white horses when she comes.
   She'll be drivin' six white horses when she comes.
   She'll be drivin' six white horses,
   She'll be drivin' six white horses,
   She'll be drivin six white horses when she comes.

3. Oh, we'll all go out to meet her when she comes.
   Oh, we'll all go out to meet her when she comes.
   Oh, we'll all go out to meet her,
   Yes, we'll all go out to meet her,
   Yes, we'll all go out to meet her when she comes.

4. She'll be wearin' a blue bonnet when she comes.
   She'll be wearin' a blue bonnet when she comes.
   She'll be wearin' a blue bonnet,
   She'll be wearin' a blue bonnet,
   She'll be wearin' a blue bonnet when she comes.

Traditional

This Old Man

Traditional

1. This old man,   he played one,   he played knick - knack   on   my drum. ⎫ With a
2. This old man,   he played two,   he played knick - knack   on   my shoe. ⎭

3.-10. *(See additional lyrics)*

Chorus

knick - knack pad - dy - whack, give the dog a bone, this old man came roll - ing home.

Additional Lyrics

3. This old man, he played three
   He played knick-knack on my knee. *Chorus*

4. This old man, he played four,
   He played knick-knack on my door. *Chorus*

5. This old man, he played five,
   He played knick-knack on my hive. *Chorus*

6. This old man, he played six,
   He played knick-knack on my sticks. *Chorus*

7. This old man, he played seven,
   He played knick-knack up to heaven. *Chorus*

8. This old man, he played eight,
   He played knick-knack at the gate. *Chorus*

9. This old man, he played nine,
   He played knick-knack on my line. *Chorus*

10. This old man, he played ten,
    He played knick-knack over again. *Chorus*

Splish Splash

Words and Music by
BOBBY DARIN
and MURRAY KAUFMAN

With a beat

Splish splash, I was tak - in' a bath ____ 'long a - bout - a Sat - ur - day night. A rub dub, just re -
Bing bang, I saw the whole gang ____ danc - in' on my liv - in' room rug. Flip flop, they were

lax - in' in the tub, think - in' ev - 'ry - thing was all right. Well, I
do - in' the bop, all the teens ___ had the danc - in' bug. There was

stepped out the tub, put my feet on the floor, I
Lol - li - pop with Peg - gy Sue, Good

Repeat and Fade

A Spoonful of Sugar

from Walt Disney's MARY POPPINS
Words and Music by
RICHARD M. SHERMAN
and ROBERT B. SHERMAN

Fast

F

In ev - 'ry job that must be done there is an el - e - ment of
feath - er - ing his nest has ver - y lit - tle time to
bees that fetch the nec - tar from the flow - ers to the

A♭dim7   C7

fun; you find the fun and snap! the job's a game; _____
rest while gath - er - ing his bits of twine and twig. _____
comb nev - er tire of ev - er buzz - ing to and fro. _____

B♭   D♭7   F

_____ And ev - 'ry task you un - der - take be - comes a piece of
_____ Though quite in - tent in his pur - suit he has a mer - ry tune to
_____ Be - cause they take a lit - tle nip from ev - 'ry flow - er that they

G7   Gm7   A♭dim7   C7   Cdim7   Gm7   Cdim7

cake, a lark! A spree! It's ver - y clear to
toot; He knows a song will move the job a -
sip, and hence, they find their task is not a

This Land Is Your Land

Words and Music by
WOODY GUTHRIE

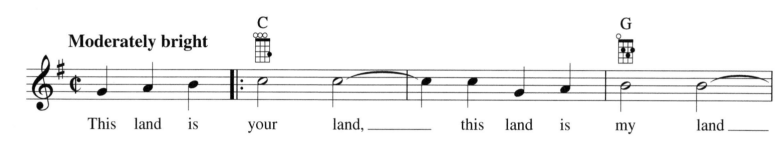

This land is your land, _____ this land is my land _____

_____ from Cal - i - for - nia _____ to the New York is - land. _____

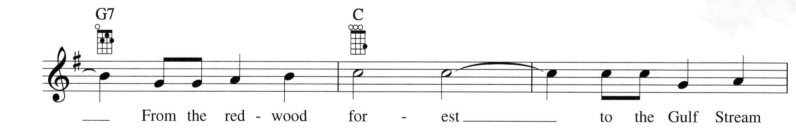

_____ From the red - wood for - est _____ to the Gulf Stream

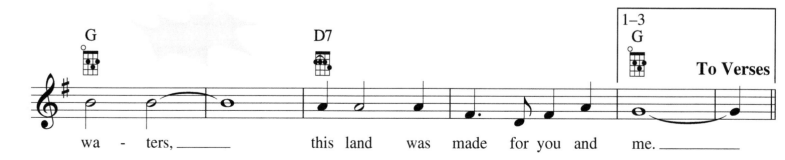

wa - ters, _____ this land was made for you and me. _____

Yellow Submarine

from YELLOW SUBMARINE
Words and Music by
JOHN LENNON
and PAUL McCARTNEY

March tempo

In the town _____ where I was born lived a man _____ who sailed the

sea. And he told _____ us of his life in the land _____ of sub-mar-

ines. So we sailed _____ up to the sun till we found _____ the sea of

green. And we lived _____ be-neath the waves in our yel - low sub - mar - ine.

We all live in a yel - low sub - mar - ine, yel - low sub - mar - ine,

Zip-A-Dee-Doo-Dah

from Walt Disney's SONG OF THE SOUTH
Words by RAY GILBERT
Music by ALLIE WRUBEL

Brightly

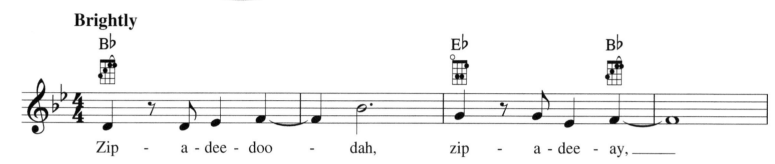

Zip - a - dee - doo - dah, zip - a - dee - ay, _____

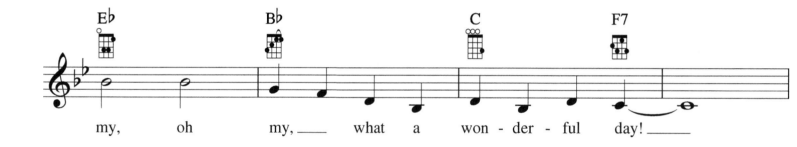

my, oh my, _____ what a won - der - ful day! _____

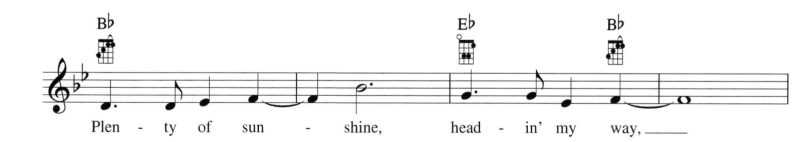

Plen - ty of sun - shine, head - in' my way, _____

Zip - a - dee - doo - dah, zip - a - dee - ay! _____ Mis - ter

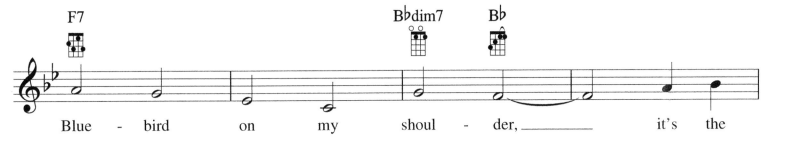

F7   B♭dim7   B♭

Blue - bird   on   my   shoul - der, _____   it's   the

C7   F7   N.C.

truth   it's   "act - ch'll,"   ev - 'ry - thing   is   "sat - is - fact - ch'll."

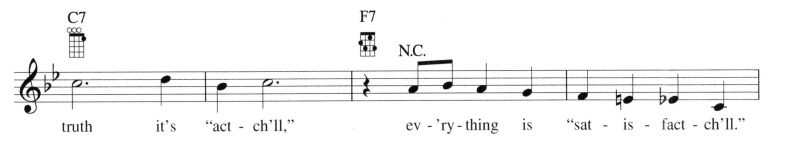

B♭   E♭   B♭

Zip - a - dee - doo - dah,   zip - a - dee - ay! ____

           E♭   B♭   Gm

____   Won - der - ful   feel - ing,

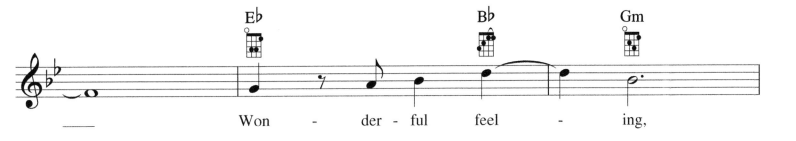

C7   F7   B♭   1.   F7   2.

won - der - ful   day. _____

Traditional

Lyrics:

1. Fa - ther and I went down to camp, a - long with Cap - tain
2. And there __ we saw a thou - sand men, as rich as Squire __
3. There __ was Cap - tain Wash - ing - ton up - on a slap - ping
4. And then __ the feath - ers on his hat, they looked so 'tar - nel
5. We saw __ a lit - tle bar - rel too, the heads were made of
6. And there __ they'd fife a - way like fun, and play on corn - stalk

Good - ing and there we saw the men and boys as thick as hast - y pud - ding.
Da - vid. And what they wast - ed ev - 'ry day, I wish it could be saved. __
stal - lion, a - giv - ing or - ders to his men, I guess it was a mil - lion.
fine, ah! I want - ed pesk - i - ly to get to give to me Je - mi - ma.
leath - er. They knocked on it with lit - tle clubs and called the folks to geth - er.
fid - dles. And some had rib - bons red as blood all bound a - round their mid - dles.

Yan - kee Doo - dle, keep it up, Yan - kee Doo - dle dan - dy.

Mind the mu - sic and the step, and with the girls be hand - y.